curious about

UFOS

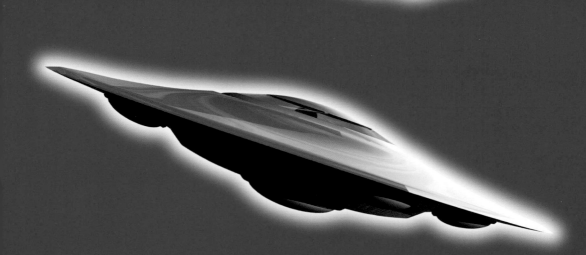

BY GILLIA M. OLSON

AMICUS • AMICUS INK

What are you

curious about?

CHAPTER THREE

3

Investigating UFOs

PAGE

16

Curious About is published
by Amicus and Amicus Ink
P.O. Box 227
Mankato, MN 56002
www.amicuspublishing.us

Copyright © 2022 Amicus.
International copyright reserved in all countries.
No part of this book may be reproduced in any
form without written permission from the publisher.

Editor: Alissa Thielges
Series Designer: Kathleen Petelinsek
Book Designers: Timothy Halldin & Ciara Beitlich
Photo researcher: Bridget Prehn

Library of Congress Cataloging-in-Publication Data
Names: Olson, Gillia M., author.
Title: Curious about UFOs / by Gillia M. Olson.
Description: Mankato : Amicus, 2022. | Series: Curious about
unexplained mysteries | Includes bibliographical references
and index. | Audience: Ages 6–9 | Audience: Grades 2–3
Identifiers: LCCN 2019056250 (print) | LCCN 2019056251
(ebook) | ISBN 9781681519845 (library binding) | ISBN
9781681526317 (paperback) | ISBN 9781645490692 (pdf)
Subjects: LCSH: Unidentified flying objects—
Juvenile literature. | Unidentified flying objects—
Sightings and encounters—Juvenile literature.
Classification: LCC TL789.2 .O58 2022 (print) |
LCC TL789.2 (ebook) | DDC 001.942—dc23
LC record available at https://lccn.loc.gov/2019056250
LC ebook record available at https://lccn.loc.gov/2019056251

Photos © iStock/MR1805 cover, 1; iStock/oorka 2 (left), 7; Alamy/
BHammond 2 (right), 14; 123rf/Igor Zhuravlov 3, 21; Shutterstock/
TukTuk Design 4; iStock/ursatii 4–5; Alamy/Chronicle 6; iStock/
Samohin 7 (plate); iStock/sjhaytov 8, 22, 23; iStock/ktsimage 9
(top); Shutterstock/IgorZh 9 (ball); Alamy/Olekcii Mach 9 (disk);
Science Source/Victor Habbick Visions 9 (triangle); Shutterstock/
Vlue 9 (diamond); iStock/mscornelius 10–11; Shutterstock/Abbie
Warnock-Matthews 13; iStock/pop_jop 15; Flickr/Phil Roeder 17;
iStock/rancho_runner 18; Wikimedia/U.S. DOD/Staff Sgt. Aaron
Allmon II 19 (F-117); Wikimedia/U.S. Air Force photo/Staff Sgt.
Bennie J. Davis III 19 (B-2 Bomber); Shutterstock/Den Rozhnovsky
19 (drones); iStock/3DSculptor 19 (satellites); iStock/Nerthuz 19
(ISS); Adobe Stock/RW-Design 20

Are UFOs real?

DID YOU KNOW?
About 1 in 6 Americans
have seen a UFO.

Any mysterious object in
the sky can be a UFO.

Yes! But UFOs don't mean aliens. UFO stands for "**unidentified** flying object." It means a strange thing was seen in the sky. Was it an alien spaceship? Probably not. Most UFOs can be explained. Some we just haven't figured out—yet.

What do UFOs look like?

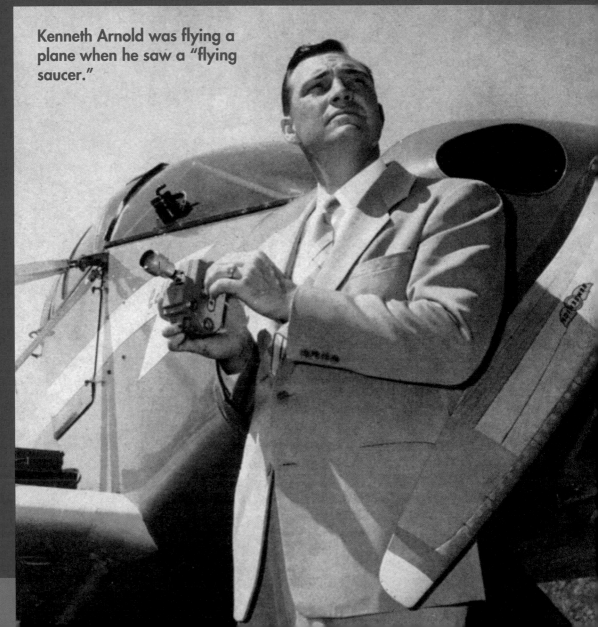

Kenneth Arnold was flying a plane when he saw a "flying saucer."

Mostly circles. In 1947, UFOs were first called "flying saucers." Kenneth Arnold saw nine flying circles. He said they flew like a skipping saucer or dish. Newspapers called them "flying saucers." The name stuck.

DID YOU KNOW?

A saucer is a small plate that holds a cup. Like the dish, flying saucers are thin and round.

A computer illustration shows how a flying saucer might look.

Do UFOs have other shapes?

Yes. People see all kinds of shapes. In 1979, an officer saw a bright ball of light. In 2004, a pilot saw an object shaped like a tube. Others have seen triangles, diamonds, or eggs!

DID YOU KNOW?
On average, the United States has about 6,000 UFO reports per year.

A drawing shows a futuristic UFO in an unusual shape.

COMMON UFO SHAPES

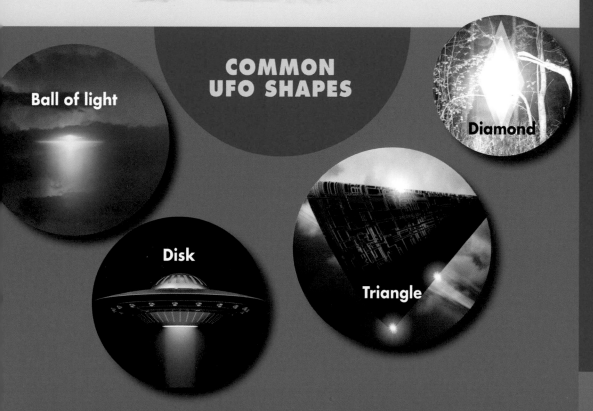

Ball of light

Diamond

Disk

Triangle

How big are UFOs?

It would be easy to spot a large UFO in a desert.

Some seem small, like a **drone**. Others seem large, like a jumbo jet. The Phoenix Lights sightings were in 1997. Thousands of people saw strange lights in the sky. Many saw a V-shaped UFO. Some people said it was a mile (1.6 km) wide.

What was the first UFO?

Ancient people saw many things they didn't understand. The first UFO record was in 214 **BC** from Rome. A man wrote about "ships in the sky." He was a historian. No one knows what he meant. Some people think he saw spaceships!

American Indians may have
also recorded UFO sightings.
This pictograph was made
hundreds of years ago in Utah.

What is the most famous UFO?

Roswell, New Mexico, is a well-known UFO-hunting area.

That might be from Roswell, New Mexico. In 1947, something crashed near the town. A nearby army base said it was an alien ship. Then they said it was a **weather balloon**. The government came clean 50 years later. It was a spy balloon they were testing.

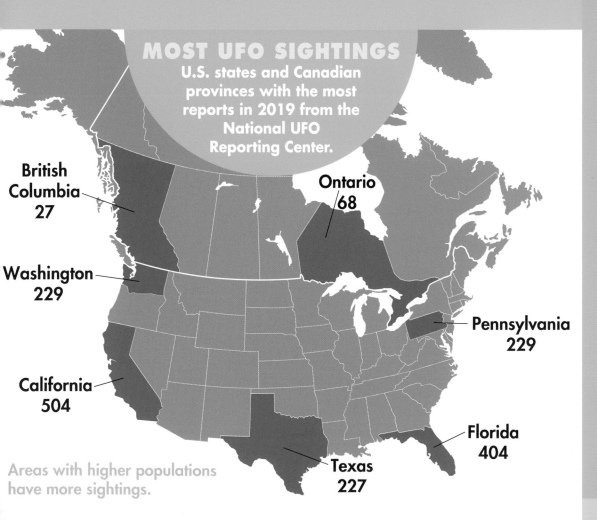

MOST UFO SIGHTINGS
U.S. states and Canadian provinces with the most reports in 2019 from the National UFO Reporting Center.

British Columbia
27

Ontario
68

Washington
229

Pennsylvania
229

California
504

Florida
404

Texas
227

Areas with higher populations have more sightings.

Who investigates UFOs?

The U.S. government. The Air Force ran Project Blue Book. From 1947 to 1969, it looked into UFO reports. From 2007 to 2012, the Department of Defense did the same. In 2019, the U.S. Navy got in the mix. Now sailors can report a sighting. There are also public groups. They get reports from people online.

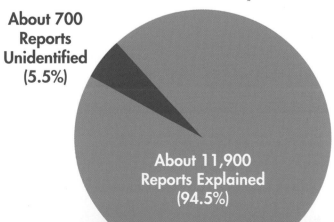

PROJECT BLUE BOOK
12,618 Total Reports

About 700 Reports Unidentified (5.5%)

About 11,900 Reports Explained (94.5%)

A depiction of lights over the U.S. Capitol that were investigated in 1952 and 2012.

Why does the government care about UFOs?

The U-2 was a new plane in the 1950s.

The object could be from another country. What if it is a spy plane? The problem is the U.S. government also tests new machines. Ever heard of Area 51? It is a secret base in Nevada. In the 1950s, the U-2 spy plane was tested there. It looked weird. It didn't move like any known plane. People thought it was a UFO!

F-117 NIGHTHAWK

B-2 BOMBER

DRONES

SATELLITES

**INTERNATIONAL
SPACE STATION**

What else could the UFOs be?

Sometimes clouds form unusual shapes.

So many things! Clouds can make weird shapes. A fireball is a blazing **meteor**. It shoots across the sky. **Sprites** are weird flashes of lightning. Some UFOs are still not explained. Who knows what we will find out?

A meteor may look like a UFO from Earth.

ASK MORE QUESTIONS

What happens at Area 51, really?

What else did they find in Project Blue Book?

Try a BIG QUESTION: If someone found scientific proof of an alien spaceship, how would that affect the world?

SEARCH FOR ANSWERS

Search the library catalog or the Internet.
A librarian, teacher, or parent can help you.

Using Keywords
Find the looking glass.

Keywords are the most important words in your question.

?

If you want to know about:

- if Area 51 has aliens, type: AREA 51 ALIENS

- what objects Project Blue Book investigated, type: PROJECT BLUE BOOK FINDINGS

FIND GOOD SOURCES

Here are some good, safe sources you can use in your research.
Your librarian can help you find more.

Books
UFO Sightings
by Katie Chanez, 2020.

UFOs: Are Alien Aircraft Overhead?
by Megan Borgert-Spaniol, 2019.

Internet Sites

History | Project Blue Book Map
https://www.history.com/shows/project-blue-book/pages/ufo-sightings-location-map
The History Channel is a popular source for history. Be aware that there may be ads that try to sell things.

Wonderopolis: What is Area 51?
https://www.wonderopolis.org/wonder/what-is-area-51
Wonderopolis is a nonprofit educational website for children.

Every effort has been made to ensure that these websites are appropriate for children. However, because of the nature of the Internet, it is impossible to guarantee that these sites will remain active indefinitely or that their contents will not be altered.

SHARE AND TAKE ACTION

Make a UFO plan.
If you saw a UFO, what would you do first? How would you figure out what it was? Who would you tell?

Learn more about space.
Find an observatory. They are common at colleges and universities. Often, they have times when the public can go for free.

Ask a parent if you can stay up to watch a meteor shower.
They happen during certain times of the year.

GLOSSARY

BC The initials of "before Christ." Used to show a date that comes before the birth of Jesus.

drone An aircraft or ship without a pilot on board that is controlled by remote.

meteor A small space rock that falls through Earth's atmosphere, which makes it burn brightly.

sprite A type of lightning that looks like a circle in the sky, with trailing lights.

unidentified Unknown.

weather balloon A balloon sent into the sky to collect weather data.

INDEX

About the Author

Gillia M. Olson is a skeptic by nature but loves all things paranormal nonetheless. She stays curious and open-minded and hopes you will, too. She lives in southern Minnesota with her husband and daughter.